Peter Müller met Fermín in 1991 when he was taking pictures of *trajes de luce*, the embroidered costumes worn by bullfighters, for his book *España por dentro* (Spain from within). Since then, the photographer, so impressed with the colors, the motifs and the perfection of each "suit of lights," has clung to the idea of publishing a new book, one dedicated to an art like no other, and one that honors one of its great designers: Fermín, couturier for bullfighters.

Spread on previous page:

Bullfighting talk around
Fermín at the restaurant
"Los Borrachos de Velásquez."
Antonio Chenel "Antoñete"
Julio Aparicio, Sr.
Miguel Flores
Fermín Lopez
Pedrucho de Canarias
Enrique Bernedo "Bojilla".

ORO PLATA

EMBROIDERED COSTUMES OF THE BULLFIGHT

Photographs
Peter Müller

Danièle Carbonel
based on text by *Pedro Soler*

Preface
Luis Miguel Dominguín

ASSOULINE

There is no blood or tragedy in
this book. Herein lies, as I have
seen it, the most magical aspect
of the bullfight: the "suit of
lights." The matadors are in gold,
the "cuadrillas" in silver. Most of
the suits were designed by Fermín
to whom I dedicate this book.
Without his help, the soul of this
"faena" would not exist.

PETER MÜLLER

ORO PLATA

EMBROIDERED COSTUMES OF THE BULLFIGHT

Preface

Salmon colored, embroidered, white silk, the pants were very short. They were lightweight, practical and supple, suitable for a small, slight ten year old. This was my first "suit of lights."

When I saw it draped on the chair, I had a feeling I was meeting my lifelong companion. Even before putting it on to go to the arena, I would speak to it: "You see, we are alone here you and I, while outside lies the world that we will conquer!"

This feeling stayed with me during my whole career.

One day, someone asked me what the "suit of lights" means to me. "It's my second skin," I answered spontaneously. Sometimes it seems that my suit experiences the most intense feelings with me: fear, failure and triumph. Of everything that is outside of me, it is what I am closest to. The color of the silks and the dazzle of the sequins blend into the ornamentation of the costume that hovers between the magical and the liturgical.
It is a suit that demands character. Whoever wears it is bestowed with certain abilities that other fineries do not offer.

The suit, like all inanimate objects, is cold and indifferent. It is no more than the hazy outlines of an imagined image, or a tongue that speaks random words. But against the body of a bullfighter, tight against his muscles and highlighting his veins, its hidden reality is revealed. It takes on a life of its own; it becomes indispensable.

For what is a torero without his costume? How can he perform one perfect pass after another if the suit's satin and sparkle do not detect the proximity of the bull's horns? Without this sixth sense, neither the bullfighter nor the art of bullfighting would be the same.

The range of colors are like destiny. There will always be someone who at the end of the evening will attribute any mishap to the blue, garnet, green or yellow of a suit.

Other superstitions often tacitly emerge, becoming a psychological part of a victory.

My body bears the scars of sixteen horn stabs.

Though I have never associated my wounds with the colors of my suit, let me briefly tell you a story: I was in a bullfight in Melilla, for which I wore a certain purple and gold suit for the first time. I was gored in the thigh by the bull. I gave the new suit to my brother Pepe and he was gored in Algeciras. Pepe passed it on to a "novillero" (novice) in Saragossa. He was gored! The suit was nothing but a hand out, wandering from ring to ring, worn in less and less impressive circles, and each time it left blood and tragedy behind it.

So I say no to purple! Maybe it has something against me, I'll never know. But it is better to keep away from it. It can't hurt. Besides, there are so many other colors to choose from!
Perhaps every bullfighter has a "purple" in his past.

And as one eminent Galician stated, "I don't believe in witches, but I know bad luck exists!".

Luis Miguel Dominguín

Spread on previous page:

Taffeta and silk
in the Casa Fermín.

Right and overleaf:

Burgundy and gold jacket
covered by a muslin garment
protector. Late nineteenth-
century motif.

Luis Dominguín tells us that during one bullfight a plane flew overhead triggering the abrupt impression that he was of another time. He was an anachronism: the discomfort was so great he almost gave up his career. The combination of finding himself amidst a crowd of twenty thousand donned in this "suit of lights" so important in the eighteenth century, and the white tracks above marking the speed of sound was completely disorienting. Yet when he regained equilibrium, Dominguín continued with the "faena," the final part of the bullfight, and decided not to abandon his career. On the contrary, this experience allowed him to understand the unique nature of his role more clearly. He needed to grab hold of his acute difference, and find that "sosiego," the inner peace and self-mastery that the writers of the Golden Age considered the goal for all hidalgo.

That very night, while removing his lavish costume, the bullfighter looked at his past and felt grateful for this suit that calls for a noble body and soul.

Spread on previous page:
Navy blue and gold jacket. "C" motif from the end of the nineteenth century.

David Luguillano in a plum and gold suit. "LM" motif, the initials of Luis Miguel Dominguín.
Dominguín simplified an ancient design to create a new embroidery pattern.

Previous pages:

Navy blue and gold jacket. "Conch shell"
motif. The front of the jacket is decorated
with gold aglets trimmed with white silk.

Fernando Lozano
in blue and gold
pants. Original motif.

The history of the costume:
from "majo" to torero.

Why this costume?
Behind the obvious theatricality of the "traje de luces" lies Spanish history, symbolically intertwined with the birth and evolution of the costume.
At the root of it all is the burning need for dignity, a relentless desire to be equal to a nobleman, who since the Middle Ages, like the Moors, had performed bullfights on horseback. The popular adage, "En cada español, un rey!" (In every Spaniard, a king!) clearly illuminates this ambition to prove to the hidalgo, to the knight, that a common man can also aspire to valor and honor; and that this same common man can create rules for combat, a way of being, and finally, a costume.
In the eighteenth century, commoners earned the right to enter the arena's magic ring but were made to wear a sash over their chests as a sign of this privilege. Soon they were allowed to face the bull, but only on foot! Pepe Hillo, the bullfighter whose death in the arena was immortalized by Goya in an engraving, wrote the first treatise on bullfighting, *Arte de torear a pie y a caballo* (The art of bullfighting on foot and on horseback).

It was at the end of the eighteenth century, Goya's era, that the Spanish people finally brought to life the idea they had slowly been cultivating: the perfect matador.

Of course, they already had the noble "toreo" on horseback as an example, a form that came to be known as "corrida de rejón." But they were looking for something else, a dream, an exhaltation that would outshine the aristocrat's prowess.

Throughout their history, the Spanish people have questioned the relationship between life and dreams. From Don Quixote to the character of Segismundo in the play *Vida es sueth* (Life is a dream), heroes have restlessly strived to make their dreams real.
Goya's work is the epitome of such a search and it is no coincidence that he portrayed both bullfighting (he was the first painter to do so) and the harsh realities of war against Napoleon. At the same time that Pepe Hillo and Francisco Romero were performing in the ring, the Spaniards were fighting the invader. Although the aristocracy remained more or less "afrancesada" (following French style) a sense of national identity seized the country, sweeping through the arenas. The new theatricality, both prestigious and seductive, that penetrated Spain's collective consciousness, and the image of the matador's suit in particular, obliterated the somber and vain gallantry of the aristocrats.

Richard Milan in dark red and gold pants. "Three branches and two bouquets" motif.

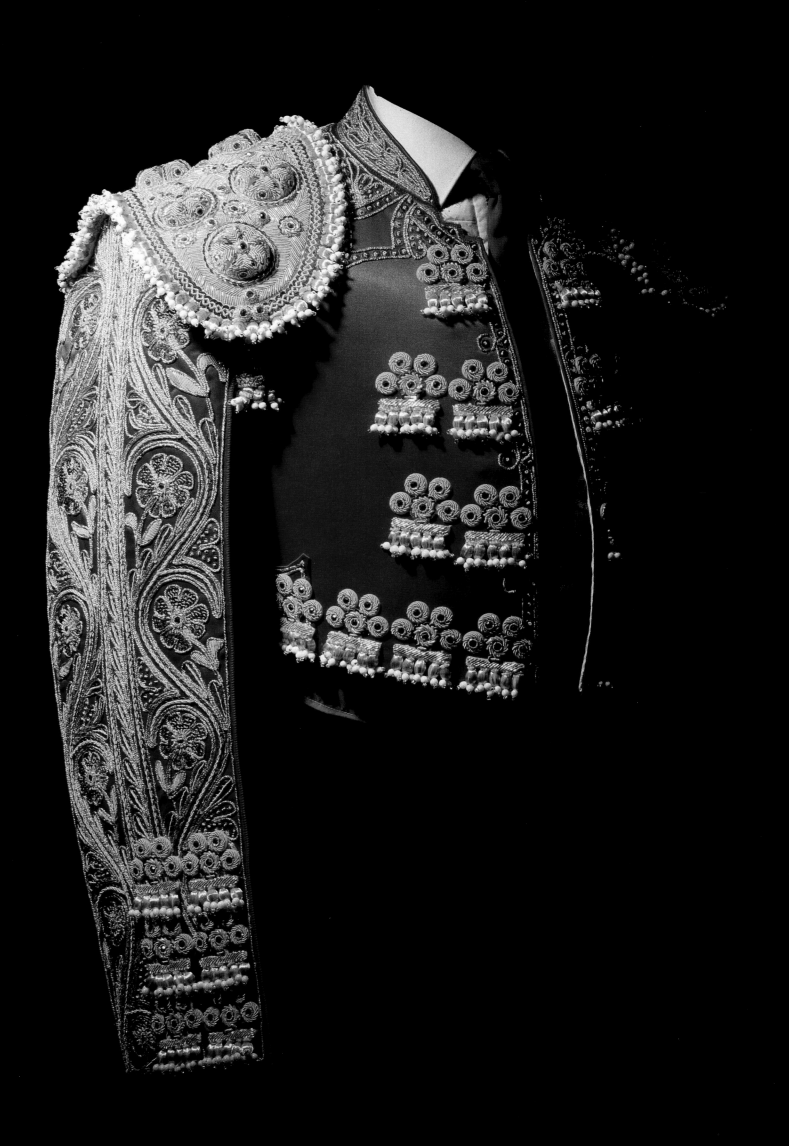

What has influenced the suit? After the somewhat coarse style of the early eighteenth century, when men wore a red sash across their chests, and leather breeches and belts, the suit became, in certain ways, more urban by borrowing from the fashion of the "majos," the Spanish aristocrats who adopted Spanish rather than French fashion. These are the same "majos" that Goya immortalizes in his tapestry cartoons.

In his work, L'*Espagne sous Ferdinand VII* (*Spain under Ferdinand* VII), the Marquis de Custine describes how taken he is with the sartorial refinement of the young Madrileneans:

"There are the elegant ones on the street referred to as 'majos'. The most important lords do not deign to imitate them. Others dress in short breeches and embroidered leather gaiters which are left open around the calf. They are not without grace.

"Others still, the most refined, are dressed in velvet jackets decorated with little tufts of silk and gold aglets (...)

"The dress and character of each man are full of surprises and are subjects to be studied here."

In Goya's famous portrait of Francisco Romero, it is this apparel that the sitter is wearing. On his mighty head rests the elegant, almost feminine velvet cap that the bullfighters wore before the famous "montera."

The transition is made from "majo" to matador, from dandy to idol, from profane elegance to sacred elegance.

Fabrics became more and more precious. Leather and woolen cloth were replaced by silk, and where previously the bright colors had been embroidered with velvet or cord, the suit was now decorated with shining gold ornamentation and arabesques. Only the matador – the one who actually kills the bull – was allowed to don gold, while his assistants, whether banderilleros or picadors, wore silver. This shift to gold was a first step into a mythical world. For not only does the matador become the "lord" of the popular game, but he also enters the world of the sacred. For who else in Spain could be seen in this excessive splendor save the statues of saints bearing richly adorned chasubles that are paraded through the streets during religious holidays?

José María Manzanares, draped in a white "capote de paseo" (entrance cape) with trimming. Blue and gold suit. "Vase" motif.

In this Spain, both so Catholic and so pagan, it never seemed blasphemous to turn a gladiator who fought beasts into an idol. First and foremost, the bullfighter, as opposed to the gladiator, was a free man who could withdraw from the game if he so desired by cutting his "coleta" (pigtail), the mark of his caste. A second reason was that he received a salary as well as gifts. The most influential ladies of the court, such as the Duchess of Albe, considered it an honor to offer the bullfighter the most handsome "suit of lights," just as they provided the finery for the statues of saints. Finally, a third and essential reason, is that the bullfighter offers his life to other men. He takes the ultimate risk and, in certain ways, grants social redemption to a people hungry for honor.

The sacred aspect is easily absorbed into the collective unconscious, and it is no coincidence that so many bullfighters had and still have the tragic effigy embroidered on their ceremonial capes known as "Cristo del Gran Poder," or "Almighty Christ," the Byzantine icon in whose footsteps he follows. The people accept these origins, this subtle and unconscious blend of influences, though they like to turn a blind eye to the fact that this passion for bulls has roots in the depths of time, in the mysterious Mithraic cults and even the splendid cave paintings of Altamira.

The Spanish people made an easy transition – like a well performed pass – from the profane to the sacred, because it was engrained in their soul. A simple explanation, perhaps, but one that accounts for much!

We are now far from the shallow appreciation that a novice spectator first has of the "cuadrilla" when they appear in the arena, shining in the sunlight. Wrapped in satin, gold and gems, their capes draped Roman style around them, they carefully walk out onto the silky sand, right foot first, and make the sign of the cross. The bullfighters have a strange rendezvous with the public, out under the sun, at the center of an age-old arena, where both light and shadow fight for their share of space. They met their first challenge a long time ago, but nevertheless, face it again every day. In a time dominated by the slovenly and the pretentious, in a time when everyone has gone plebeian, this ritual and the suits donned by its performers still have the power to fascinate. In the beginning the right to combat, as well as the right to wear this suit, represented a people's challenge to prove their nobility. Now the fight stands against what reigns with impunity over us all: vulgarity, banality, and the commonplace.

Spread on previous page:

Center of a "capote de paseo" richly decorated in silk embroidery.

Luis Francisco Esplá. Midnight blue suit, embroidered with jet. Late seventeenth-century design.

Antonio Borrero "Chamaco."
Tobacco brown and gold suit.
"C" motif from the end of the
nineteenth century.

Rui Bento in a purple and
gold suit. "Vase" motif.

Pepe Luis Martín
in a green suit embroidered
with jet. Late seventeenth-
century "pine cone" motif.

Don Fermín, couturier for bullfighters.

We must give credit where credit is due. In a book about the "suit of lights" the artisans cannot be left unmentioned. But this title is belittling; let us call them artists, even though many couturiers for bullfighters would modestly shy away from such ranking. A bullfighter's suit, it should be noted, requires more than a month of work, not including the preparation period in which the colors, the embroidery and the materials, among other things, are chosen. Many fittings are also required.

The costume is perfectly tailored, every cut is exact so there is not one false fold. Tradition dictates that during the fight the torero must remain impeccable, "sin despeinarse, ni mancharse" (hair unruffled, clothes unsullied). This of course is quite a challenge, and a perfect fit is one of the essential factors in the success of an outstanding costume. There have of course been great couturiers for bullfighters since the beginning of the nineteenth century, but in recent decades many of the big ateliers have disappeared. In Seville, for example, where the incomparable "Maestranza" bullring is situated, the Casa Manfredi and the Casa Celis have closed. There is no one left in Barcelona! Most of the great couturiers now work out of Madrid.

In this country where the guild system was only established recently, corporations play an important role. The vocation is often passed from father to son; certain women also follow the profession, like "La Nati" (her mother was in the trade before her). This is rare, however.

Even though almost all suits are made according to traditional rules, those familiar with the art can distinguish a Justo Albaga from a Santiago Pelayo. But the most famous designer of them all – although he will deny it – is Don Fermín. He is the art incarnate, and has been involved in the world of bullfighting since his youth when "se visitío de corto." In other words, he wore the bullfighter's elegant civilian clothing – straight pants and short jacket – just like the matadors who wear them on social occasions to be distinguished from the uniformity of style around them.

Spread on previous page:

Sebastián Palomo Linares
in front of one of his paintings.

Víctor Méndes in a
burgundy velvet and gold
suit with flower motif.

Who is Don Fermín?
He's rather round physically, and has the air of someone important; he's warm and observant. He works and receives clients in a quiet, opulent house near the Gran Vía in Madrid.

His mother was an embroiderer who, according to Fermín's brother Antonio, often worked into the early hours of the morning to support her family. It was the post-war era, with its rations and the black market. Even at this time, the young Fermín mingled with the bullfighting crowd, counting Antoñete and Julio Aparicio among his friends. However, he attained his dream of heroism in a different way – by becoming a "sculptor of light." His modest beginnings were with the Casa Ripolles, one of the best-known studios in Madrid at the time. Thirty years later he is firmly established, and dresses all the best, from Dominguín to Espartaco and El Cordobés.

He is known for his unrivaled talent for the perfect cut and his sense of esthetic harmony. Despite the fact that he has thirty employees in his studio, he designs each costume personally, choosing the colors, selecting and drawing the embroidery himself. Familiar with the career of each client, his advice depends on the place of the fight, the bullfighter's age, style, and even his mood of the moment.

Like a knight in a tournament, the bullfighter often wears a color or an embroidery like an emblem, signifying his membership to a sort of bullfighting nobility.

The challenge for the couturier is to innovate within a genre that is, fundamentally, extremely traditional. And this requires talent!

Despite certain fixed forms and rules, the suit can change subtly and ingeniously. Twenty years ago, there was a tendency, for convenience's sake, to limit embellishments and embroidery. Over recent years, however, bullfighters like Luis Francisco Esplá, for whom esthetics are important, have influenced a return to a more ornamental style.

Vincente Yesteras, banderillero in a fuchsia and silver suit. "Aztec" motif, contemporary design.

Certain details of the costume, explains Don Fermín, can be traced all the way back to the Middle Ages and to traditional Arab embroideries, arabesques, calligraphy, and luxurious caparisons. There is also some French influence which dates to the reign of Louis XIV's grandson, Philippe d'Anjou. When he became king of Spain in 1700, the court abandoned the Hapsburg penchant for dark, austere colors, adopting instead silk outfits, gems, embroidered breeches and colored tights, all which soon became part of the "suit of lights." In time, the suit evolved to adapt for use during the bullfight; "la chaquetilla" (the jacket), for example, was shortened so as not to obstruct movement.

The decoration that adorns religious sculptures was another major influence, especially on the embroidery of the "capote de paseo" which often depicts religious themes.

For a long time, the splendid embroidery for the "suits of lights" was, in a somewhat amusing paradox, sewn by nuns, like the charming "Monja gitana" (gypsy nun) described by Garcia Lorca:

"Que bien borda, con que gracia
Sobre la tela pajiza
Ella quisiera bordar
Flores de su fantasia
Que girasol, que magnolia!
De lentejulas y cintas!
Que azafranes y que lunas!
En el mantel de la misa "

"How well she embroiders,
with such grace
on the hay-colored fabric
She would like to embroider
The flowers of her fancy
Such sunflowers, such magnolias!
With sequins and cord!
What yellows, what silvers!
On the altar cloth!"

If you ask Don Fermín about the fate of the craft, he will answer that a strong future is likely. In Spain, bullfights incite great interest and are televised every Sunday during the season, helping to introduce a new generation to the "fiesta brava." Don Fermín greatly hopes that his sons will succeed him, not only because they are interested in the trade, but also because he feels he is invested with a mission to preserve a cultural tradition.

Red and gold "capote de paseo" embroidered with silk, depicting the Virgin of Guadeloupe, patron saint of Mexico.

Pedrito de Portugal
in a sky blue and gold suit
with "pine cone" motif.

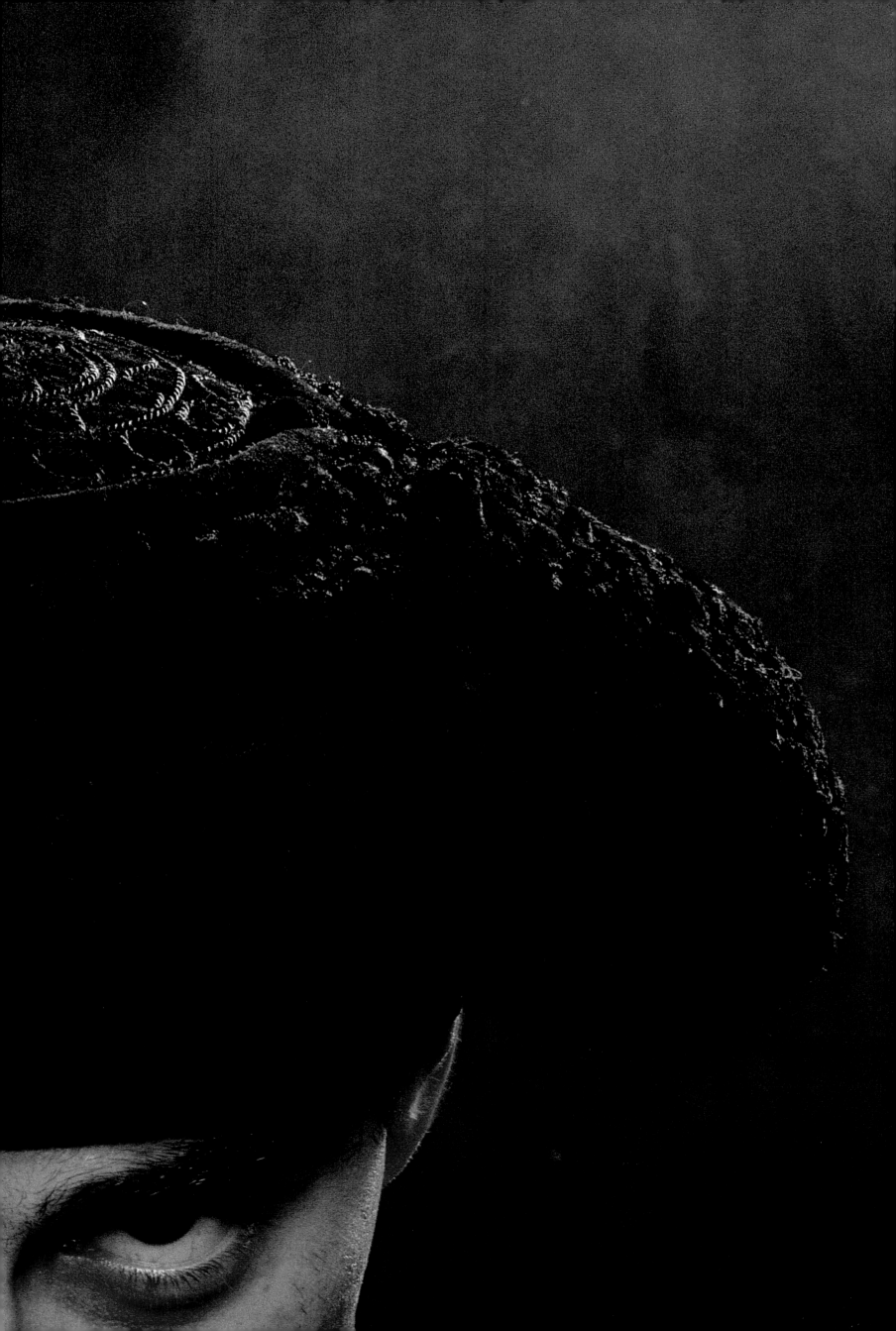

One can easily imagine the bustle in Don Fermín's studio when one considers that the most famous bullfighters, who participate in seventy or eighty bullfights a year, require six or seven suits per season. The bullfighting world has a strict hierarchy – althougha kind of natural respect predominates – and often the distinguished bullfighter, known as "la figura," supports his "cuadrilla" financially. The banderilleros don magnificent costumes as well, but they are embroidered in silver. The picadors – the riders reminiscent of nobles who were sometimes permitted to wear gold – wear big, strongly reinforced jackets, which protect them from the bull's charges. Their pants are long, similar to those worn by the "vaqueros" (bull herders). They wear genuine hinged armor over their legs joined to huge stirrups, and a round hat secured by a chin strap, which, as tradition has it, resembles the one worn by Don Quixote. Although the picadors appear bulky, their skill as horsemen is unrivaled.

With so many orders, the Casa Fermín is the privileged meeting place for the bullfighting circle. The studios are filled with a warm and ebullient atmostphere, particularly during the leadup to the major festivals.
When Don Fermín gave up his personal dream of becoming a matador, he became a sort of "midwife" for bullfighters. For, make no mistake, the "traje de luces" not only clothes the bullfighter, but also forms him: it sculpts him, makes him stand upright, brings him into the world for a second time.

Spread on previous page:

"Montera"(cap) de Morillas.
Antonio Borrero "Chamaco."

Right:

José Ortega Cano in garnet and gold pants. Late nineteenth-century "wave" motif.

Overleaf:

Manuel Benítez "El Cordobés."

"Suit of lights" is both a literal and a metaphorical name. Literal, because the suit is made to catch the sun; the thin gold thread, and the sequins and gems which are the base of most of the embroidery, trap the light. Up to twelve miles of gold thread can be required to complete the embroidery on certain suits! The suit must be seen from afar. The gold, whether it is "camarana," "canutillo," or "hojela," made of pure thread, fine gold, or simple copper, is the primary decoration and distinguishes the "diestro," the one who carries the sword, from his team. The bullfighter must be followed by light, so bullfights entirely in the shade are avoided where possible. In fact the bullfight often occurs at five o'clock in the afternoon, when the arena is divided between shade and light. The suit shimmers and sparkles as it travels between light and dark, making a startling contrast to the bull's dark coat.

The term "suit of lights" can also be seen as a metaphor since the bullfighter is the symbolic bearer of light. There is a strange coincidence with the word Lucifer, meaning "bearer of light," and the tragic fate of this fallen angel, but these should be left to one side – a bullfighter would cross himself at the mention! As the bull steps from the shade into the light where the bullfighter awaits him, we are reminded of the mythical battles of the great archangels, like Saint George slaying the dragon.

"Vestirse de luces," to dress in lights, is perhaps the most beautiful, poetic expression invented to describe a person dressing up for a challenge, preparing for a fight. Francisco Montes, known as "Paquiro," born in 1808, was the first to give the suit of lights a definitive form. He introduced the wonderful epaulettes that adorn the jackets, as well as the particular shape of the narrow pants, known as "taleguillas." Although a romantic and a liberal, Francisco Montes imagined his suit as something that would blaze a trail to a new kind of aristocracy. Alexandre Dumas tells us that Montes considered his participation in a bullfight, as long as it was attended by royalty, as a benediction:
"I have no need to tell you, Madame, that Montes is the king of bullfighters. Montes only performs if invited by a king, a prince or a town."
Today, comments on the suit are still likely to flatter. For example, if someone tells a man or woman "torero – toreravas", meaning "bullfighter, go!", it means they find they have the royal power of seduction attributed to a torero. Talking about the origins of the suit, Don Fermín says: "To be a bullfighter, to know that you are admired, undoubtedly stirs up a desire to be as wonderfully dressed as possible."

The "suit of lights."

The shirt, always white, is made of a fine batiste which is often discreetly trimmed with lace, giving it an almost feminine elegance. Certain bullfighters have a superstitious attachment to their shirt. It is said that Manolete wanted to keep the same shirt for his whole career, having it endlessly altered and lovingly mended.

When the horns get at and rip the shirt, the bullfighter is said to be "desvestido" (undressed); in other words, they have had a very close brush with death.

The jacket is a masterpiece in itself. Heavy – it can weigh between six and eight pounds – it is deemed an offspring of armor and the coat of mail. In fact, the skills of a goldsmith or silversmith are required even more than those of a couturier, even though the cut must be perfect. It is the jacket, which as we know was shortened at the beginning of the nineteenth century, that is embroidered with the most extravagant designs. The epaulettes are true jewels that cascade in all their splendor over both sides of the shoulder, enhancing the matador's build and slimming the waist. In general, floral, plant, and geometric patterns are chosen for the embroidery while beaded gold or pearl aglets often adorn the front of the jacket. Jet and black garnishes are used when the torero is in mourning, or when he wants to effect a more somber look, reminiscent of the

"goyescas" (eighteenth-century bullfights) of early times.
The silver embroidery that adorns the "cuadrilla's" costumes receives the same exacting attention, sophisticated decoration and perfection of cut that is bestowed on the matador's suit.

The first step in the embroidery is a life-size drawing on paper. Depending on the process of the stencil worker ("l'estarcillado"), the lines are usually poked with a needle and the holes are then filled with talc, using a stocking. When the paper is removed, an outline of the drawing remains beneath it on the cloth. A thick gold cord is then pinned along the outline, acting as the design's perimeter. Once the cloth is tacked down, the inside spaces are filled with flowers, sequins and gems, until the embroidery is completed.
The jacket is worn open, revealing a buttoned vest that is the same color as the pants. A thin tie is also worn, usually red, so that the white lace on the shirt stands out. A representation of the Virgin or the bullfighter's patron saint is sometimes pinned to the tie.

Since the end of the eighteenth century, the "taleguillas" (short pants) have been made of silk or satin. The outside of the leg is embroidered with the same motif that decorates the jacket and vest. They are worn over very close-fitting tights that protect the torero's genitalia. The tights are kept up with "machos" (garters) which are placed underneath the knee, and resemble the tassels

found hanging from the epaulettes. "Atar los machos" means to prepare for combat! Today, a new fabric known as "le punto de seda," a stretch silk, allows for more flexibility in the legs. The "taleguillas" are meant to squeeze the muscles, allowing the bullfighter to make spectacular leaps with the grace of a dancer. The tights are traditionally a bright red; only when the bullfighter is in mourning is the color changed. It is undeniable that the "taleguillas" emphasize a torero's masculinity. This aspect of the costume marks the sensuality of the fighter's dance, one of seduction and of death. Face to face with the bull, an animal replete with an undeniable sexual symbolism, the bullfighter exudes an equivalent yet more discreet and esthetic virility. The beast has his instinct, the torero has Eros.

Tobacco brown and gold vest.
"X" motif.

Spread on previous page:
Miguel Báez "Litri" (Sr.).

Juan Bellido "Chocolate," banderillero,
in a blue and silver suit. "Wave" motif.

Right:

Ricardo Ortiz in a white and gold suit.
Gold aglets trimmed with black silk.
"Aztec" motif.

Overleaf:

Javier Vázquez in a blue and gold suit.
Gold aglets trimmed with white silk.
"Vase" motif.

The "capote de paseo," or the ceremonial entrance cape, made of heavy silk or satin is a true masterpiece. The torero wears it when entering the arena, draped across his left shoulder, across his chest and around his waist. The cape is decorated with the most sophisticated embroidery, and also the most sacred.

Traditionally, the bullfighter lays the cape in front of the stalls at the feet of a person he wishes to honor. Later on, he might offer certain of these splendid garments to a Holy Virgin who has protected him. It is for this reason that the Virgin of Macarena is often depicted wearing the cape of a famous torero as a skirt.

The "brega" cape, used during the "faena" (the final third of the bullfight) is much more simple. Usually pink or yellow, it is very heavy so that it cannot be blown about by the wind. The ease with which the bullfighter performs should not fool us as to the difficulty of such athleticism!

The "montera," the cap that Francisco Montes made famous when he abandoned the original velvet cap, is worn low down over the forehead. The Casa Fermín continues to make them the traditional way, following Morillo's method that uses 2,500 small woolen knots. In the past, some bullfighters wore caps made of astrakhan, but the current "montera," as designed in the Casa Fermín, is a genuine wonder of craftsmanship. Completing one requires such sustained work that the couturier can take no more than four or five orders per year! The torero, however, will keep the same "montera" for his entire career and will often offer it to his son or a close friend who wishes to become a bullfighter.

The torero wears his cap when entering the arena, and removes it to salute the authorities, the public, and often a chosen individual to whom he dedicates the bull; this is known as the "brindis", or dedication.

Spread on previous page:

Antonio Borrero "Chamaco" (Sr.).

Center decoration of a "capote de paseo." Pink flower embroidered in red silk.

Creating these costumes requires an overall vision, which is why Don Fermín oversees every detail of a suit's design.

The choreography of bullfighting requires complete physical mastery of its technique. The torero's supple muscles and nerves of steel are under the suit's protection; the suit is his servant. As in dance, bullfighting is about combining physcial strength with grace; the difference is that one false step costs blood. Hence the loyalty that links the bullfighter to his couturier, who acts both as partner and protector, and the keeper of an entire tradition.

Don Fermín must sometimes feel he is the guardian angel of these often injured bodies, but this is a private domain of which little is told to the outside world.

Right:

Detail of a white and silver jacket. Motif from the end of the seventeenth century.

Spread on following page:

Antonio José Galán.

Spread on previous page:

Back of a white and silver jacket.
Late nineteenth-century "C" motif.

Miguel Espinosa "Armillita Chico"
wearing white and silver vest
and pants. Contemporary "branches
and pine cone" motif.

Juan Mora in a burgundy and
gold velvet suit. "Aztec" motif.

Spread on previous page:
Luis Miguel Dominguín.

José Alba "Cotón," picador in a
white jacket embroidered with black
silk. Original motif.

Choosing a suit.

One might think that, once dressed, the bullfighter focuses only on his fight, but in fact quite the contrary is true. His mood has influenced his choice of fabric from among the hundreds of colors which make up the traditional palette – one even a painter would dream about: crimson, turquoise, garnet, midnight blue, mauve, as well as the full range of grays – "burnt shadow," "merry widowers," or "London fog" – not forgetting "Soraya green," in honor of the beautiful Empress Soraya. We are reminded of the tradition of the "Merveilleuses," those elegant women of the French Directory (1795-1799), who referred to the "thigh of flushed nymph" when evoking light pink.

The torero has listened not only to his mood, but also to his fears. Each bullfighter has his own list of taboo colors, based on bad bullfights, an injury or a disconcerting past experience. Yellow is infamous for bringing unhappiness. The bullfighter will often match his suit with his "cuadrilla's" costumes. The overall picture must be perfect. Like the Catholic liturgy, which asks that a priest wear a certain color for each holiday, a bullfighter might choose his suit for a specific occasion (the Rocío pilgrimage and the pilgrimage of San Fermín, for example) since bullfights are often performed on religious holidays. White, on the other hand, is traditionally left for the "alternativa" ceremony, in which, the young "novillero", or novice,

kills the adult bull for the first time, protected by and alternating with a more experienced matador. It is a moving ceremony that recalls the medieval dubbing of knights.

In the ring, the torero never forgets what he represents, and this is inextricably linked to the suit he wears.

Triptych:

Morenito de Maracay and his "cuadrilla."

"Paroles de toreros":
first-hand accounts from three
bullfighters.

Luis Miguel Dominguín.

Dominguín dominated the
bullring from the 1950s through
the 1970s. Moreover, he was
involved in the arts and high
society during that time, a period
when a taste for Spain and
bullfighting was spreading once
again across Spanish borders.
Both Picasso and Cocteau
attended bullfights in Mougins,
and France was greatly enthused
by the writing of García Lorca.
Dominguín's love life was also the
talk of the town; his name was
uttered in the same breath as that
of the magnificent Ava Gardner,
and he eventually married the
passionate Italian actress, Lucia
Bose. Although he was a friend of
Franco, he was also a close friend
of Picasso who drew for him and
to whose home he used to go
when recuperating from injuries.
The confident Luis Miguel
Dominguín put forth his vision of
the suit and will go down in
history as a bullfighter-innovator.
In 1970 he appeared in Alicante in
a suit of lights reminiscent of
Harlequin's costume, perhaps in
reference to Picasso's famous
series of paintings on this theme.
At the same time, he perfected a
suit that was more comfortable,
and that could be put on in a few
minutes instead of the usual forty-
five! The sleeves are loose but are
lined in the same color as the
jacket so that the white of the
shirt cannot be seen. The vest is
attached to the jacket in a way
that, when buttoned, the two are
perfectly aligned. These details
were introduced to maintain the
bullfighter's neat appearance
during the fight. No movement,
however abrupt, can alter the
perfect hang of each article. This
was not Dominguín's only
innovation. Once he rushed an all
white "capote de paseo" to the
artist Alberti, for the latter to
paint as he wished. Within a
couple of hours Alberti's work was
complete, and the cape was
immediately sent back!

Did Dominguín provoke this world
of tradition? He agrees that he
was a somewhat controversial
figure. Those who watched him in
the ring, however, remember a
dazzling bullfighter of the classical
school, one who, unlike certain
famous toreros less respectful of
tradition, never indulged in
flamboyant, crowd-pleasing
passes.

Friend to artists, Dominguín knew
how to mix the esthetic concerns
of the time with the tradition he
respected. He was the first person
to realize, or at least the first who
dared to pronounce (even though
his predecessors may of thought
so before him), that "the bullfight
is like a ballet," and that, "a good
'faena' is like an orgasm." Though
shocking at the time, these
thoughts are much less so today.

José Castilla, banderillero.
Mauve and silver vest and pants.
"Oval" motif from the mid-nineteenth
century.

Right:

Pepe Ibáñez, banderillero.
Lilac and silver suit with black silk
trimming. "56" motif, designed
in 1956.

Overleaf:

Black and gold "rejoneo" jacket.
"LM" motif (Luis Miguel Dominguín).
From the collection of Ramón Serrano
(Mexico).

Luis Francisco Esplá.

When Esplá manoeuvres his "banderillas" (dowels) it is a moment of perfect elegance, skill and poetry! He is one of the few young matadors to use "banderillas," along with Victor Mendes and a couple of others. And he has never missed. The poet Manuel Machado described himself as a "Apollo's banderillero," a title to which Esplá could easily lay claim.

He is one of a generation for whom the idea of "entering the ring to escape poverty" is a veritable legend. He studied fine art and photography which greatly influenced his view of bullfighting. For him, the suit must accentuate a svelte silhouette, the embroidery should elongate the legs, and the shortened jacket should lighten the volume of the head, thereby creating "an athletic ideal in which masculinity is not hidden, but beautified and accentuated."
Having studied the history of the bullfighter's suit in depth, Esplá decided to bring back – after a period of austerity, – the highly ornamental style which had been so popular in the previous century. He also insists on wearing the vest that others, in the name of comfort, have begun to abandon.
He chooses his colors like an artist, avoiding green, which doesn't flatter his coloring, and pale, watered-down colors. He prefers strong tones, warm or cool, that stand out in the ring. Esplá can delight in the fact that today many bullfighting *aficionados* take a real interest in the suit. "I did all of this because I enjoyed it, and ever since special attention has been paid to the suit. People have started to love it again, which is surely the most important thing."

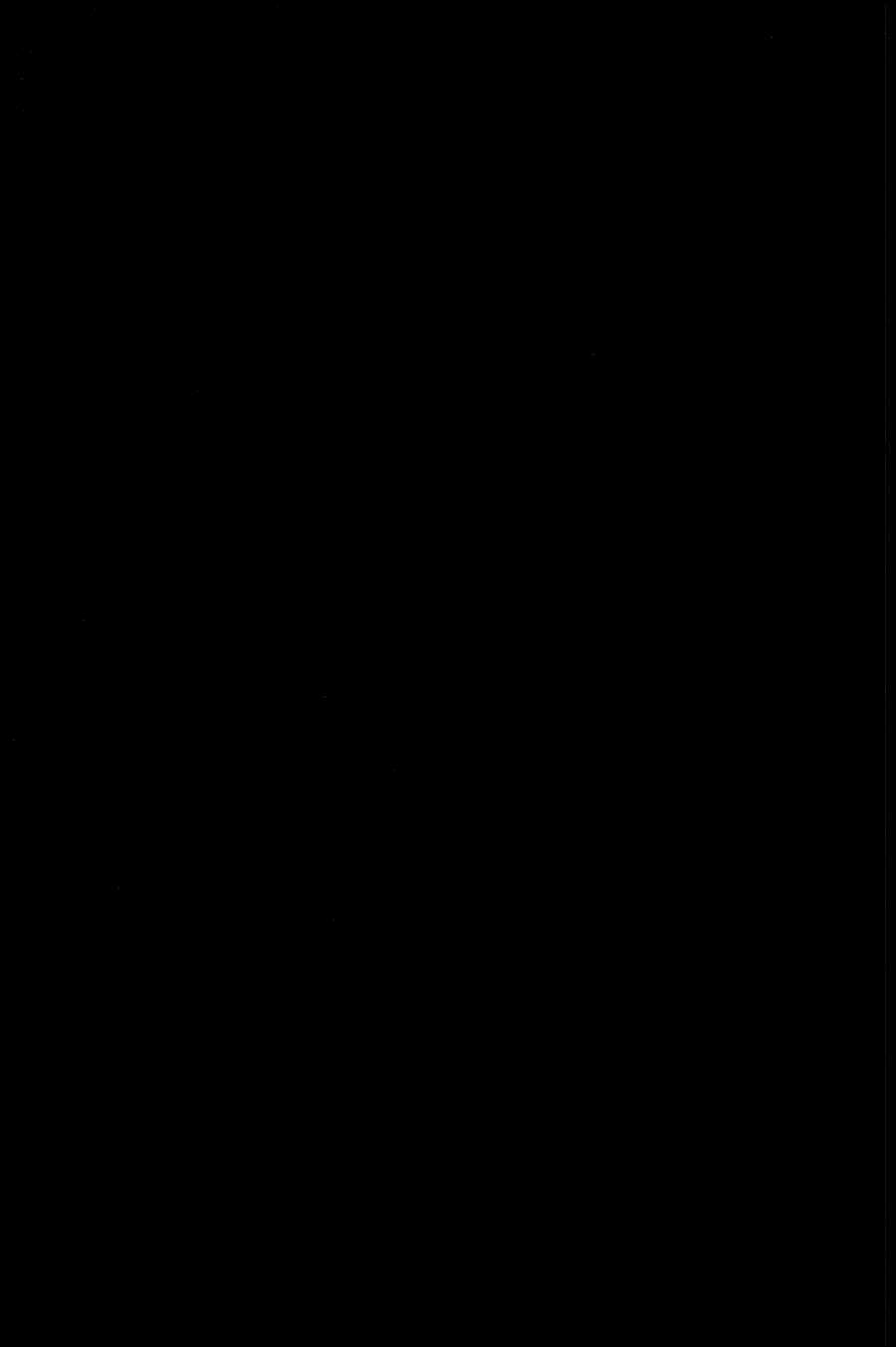

Triptych:

Enrique Ponce and his "cuadrilla."

Overleaf:

Julio Robles.

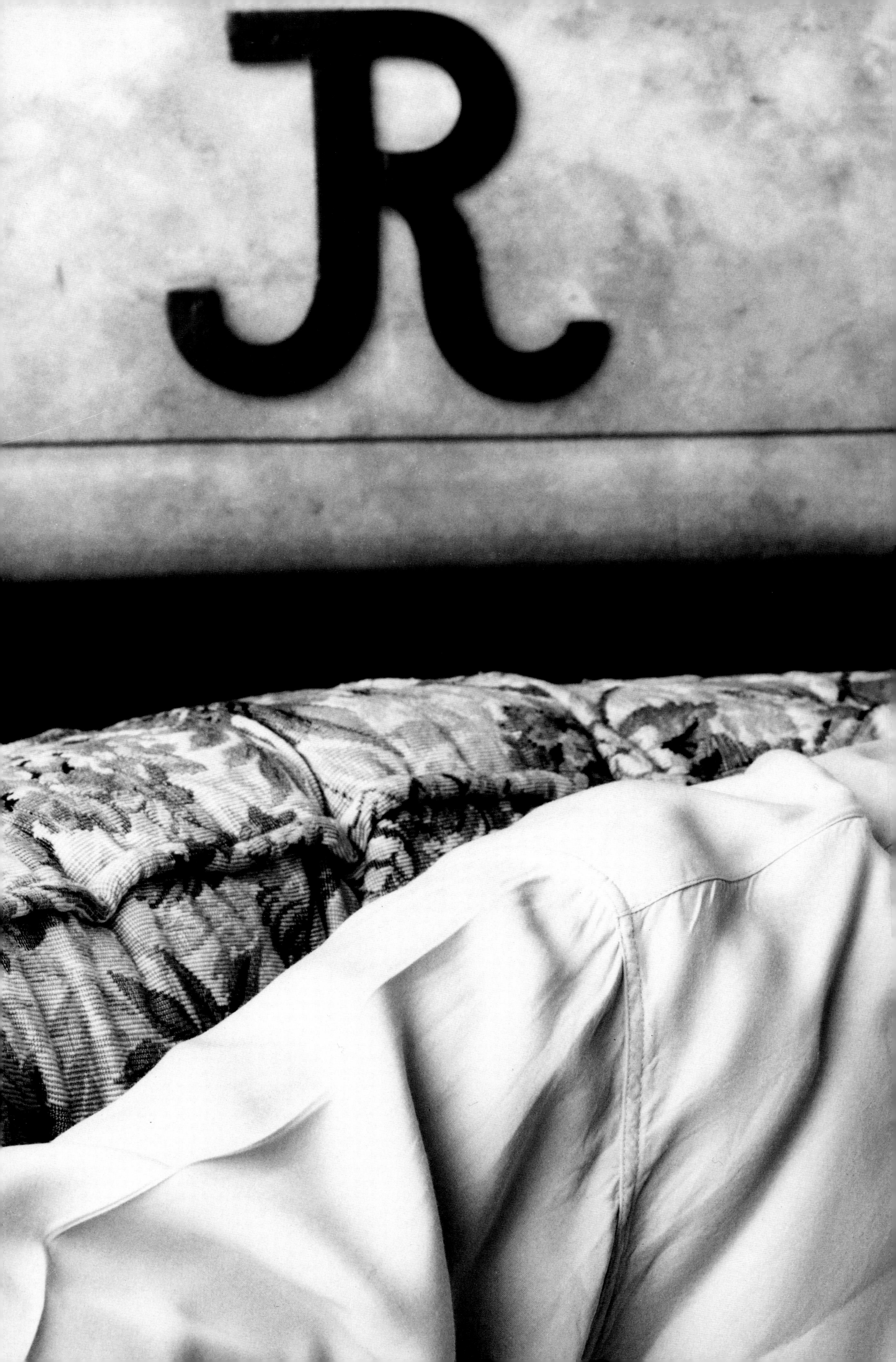
R

Right:

Rafael Corbelle, banderillero.
Green and silver suit.
Contemporary "shell" motif.

Overleaf:

Rafi Camino. Blue and gold suit.
Contemporary "bee" motif.

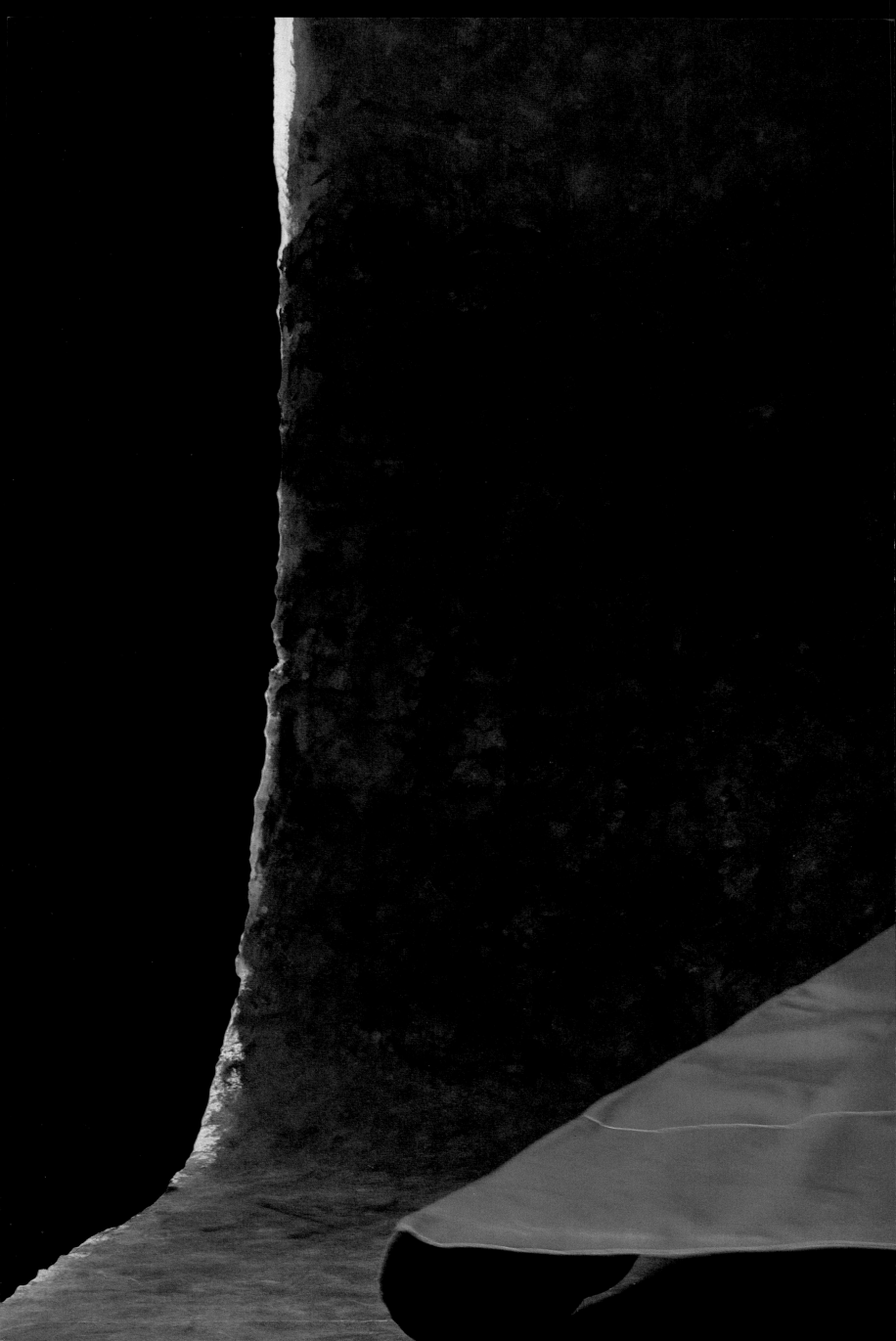

El Cordobés.

In the 1970s, El Cordobés was by
far the most famous bullfighter in
France. His showy performances,
both intriguing and popular,
thrilled the crowds.
For years he struggled,
impoverished, as a "maletilla" (an
aspiring bullfighter) and a
member of the matador's team.
He was alone. So when he finally
moved on to take part in the
"alternativa" ceremony, he could
hardly believe it! He rented a suit
which cost him twenty "duros,"
and though it was torn, the night
before the ceremony he couldn't
take his eyes off it. It was at this
moment, he says, that he truly
became a bullfighter. He adds
impulsively, "I put it on, took it off,
put it on again. I didn't think that I
would ever reach this moment in
my lifetime."
Even though Don Fermín tells
beginners that "it's not the suit
that will get you the bull's ear"
(the reward for an excellent
performance), the experience of
El Cordobés demonstrates the
profound relationship between
the bullfighter and his costume.

Spread on previous page:

Julio Aparicio and Antonio Chenel "Antoñete."

Right and overleaf:

César Rincón's suit
after a bullfight in Seville.
"Pineapple" motif.

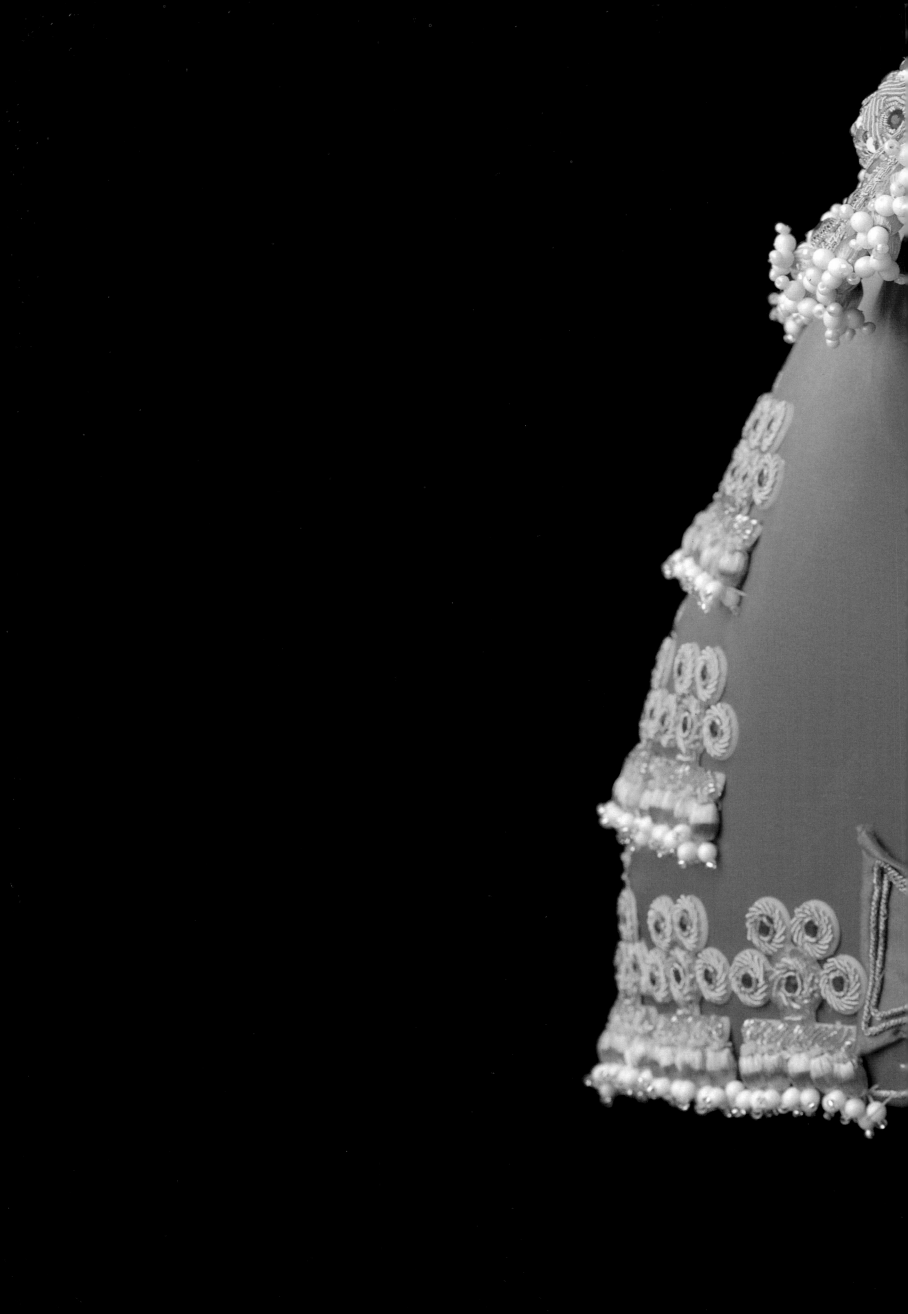

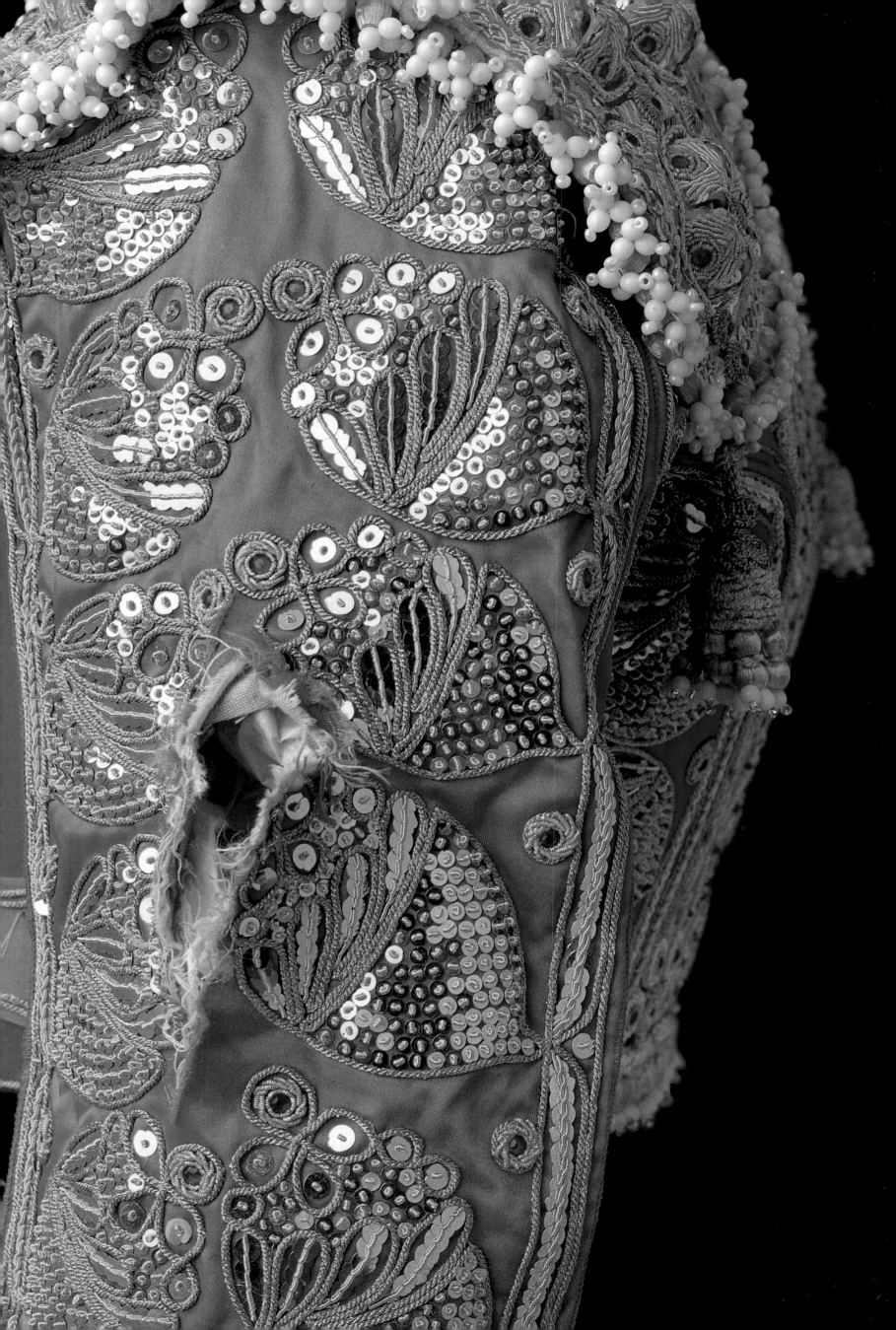

The ritual of dressing.

A few hours before the bullfight, the torero rests in the shady corners of the hotel to which he has retreated, while his "mozo de espada" (valet and sword handler) prepares the suit. Bullfighters hate to be photographed at this moment and the ceremony is rarely recorded.

The "mozo de espada" is responsible for a precious ensemble: the suit, the leather sword case, and the small case in which the cap and pigtail are kept. It is his job to lay out the suit, first preparing the "silla" (chair) which is a ritual in itself. On the back of the chair he places the suspenders, the belt, the tights, the tie, the shirt and the jacket; arranged on the seat are the "taleguillas," with the "montera" on top. Finally, the "capote de paseo" is laid over the whole. The soft pumps, made to grip to the sand in the ring, are carefully placed on the floor.

The grooming begins two or three hours before the fight. Occasionally, privileged individuals are allowed to stay during the rite, but women are excluded. The torero's face must be perfectly smooth, and he therefore gives himself a close shave. Once the ablutions have been completed, the ceremony can begin.

There is a precise order to follow which can on no account be changed. It begins with the placement of "la coleta," the lock of hair, which today is fake, to the back of the neck. According to Dominguín, this is the moment when "you sense what you must do. You dress slowly to prepare yourself, you slip on the suit, and your mindset evolves at the rhythm that will ready you for the fight."

White and gold jacket.
Gold aglets trimmed with jet.

Right:

Angel Luis Bienvenida.

Overleaf:

José Antonio Ruiz "Espartaco,"
in a lilac and gold suit.
"LM" motif (Luis Miguel Dominguín).

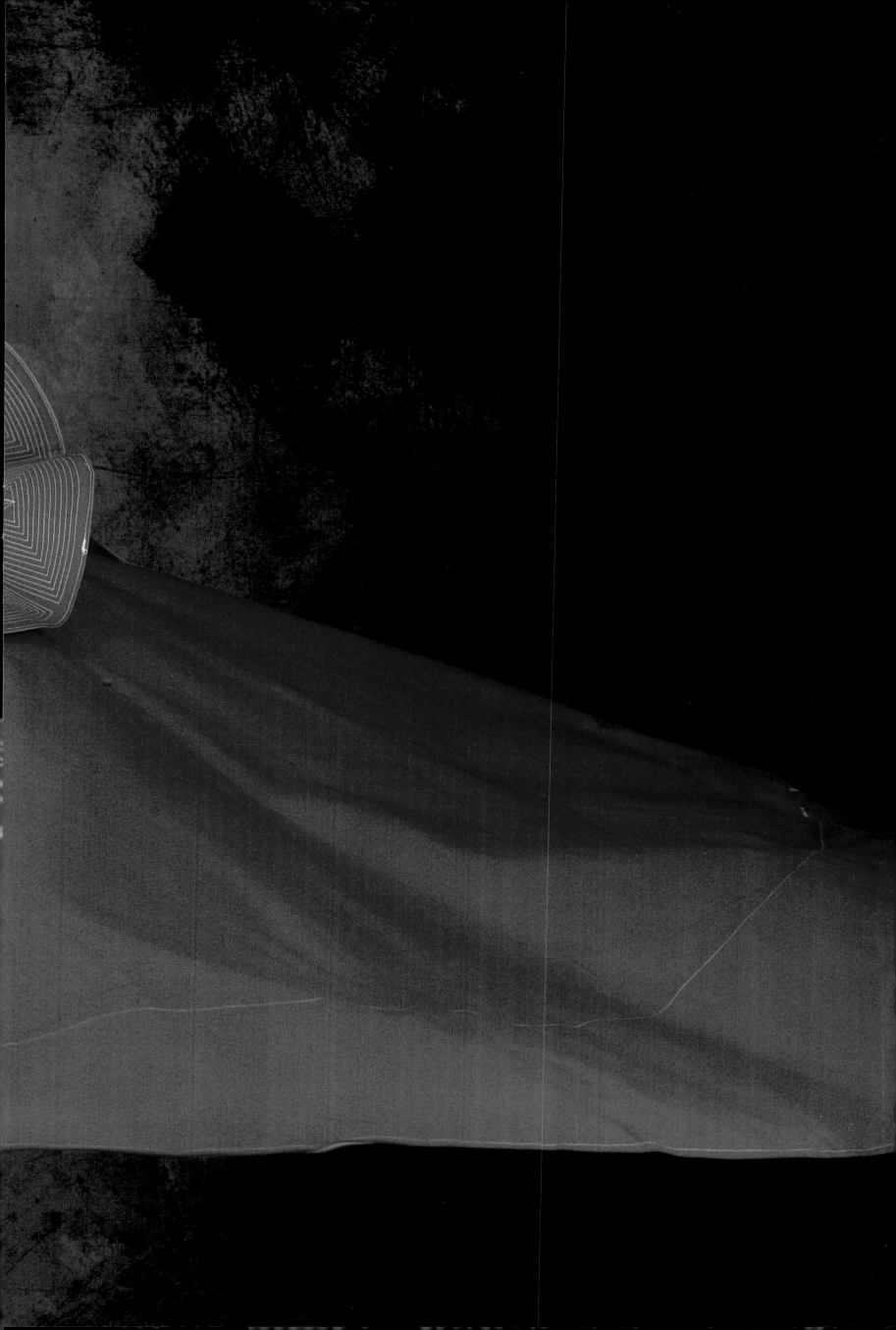

Don Fermín's brother Antonio – a regular at the ceremony – says that the experience is practically religious. It is for this reason that the bullfighters are reluctant to don their "suit of lights" except for a fitting or a bullfight. It took considerable powers of persuasion to entice the bullfighters to be photographed for this book. Putting on the suit is, for them, a secret rite.

The ritual – "El duro" (the lasting one) as it is commonly known nowadays – is slow not only because the suit is tricky to put on, but because dressing is also a time of mental preparation. Its similarity to Mass, and other religious services, has struck numerous writers, as Cocteau's *La Corrida du Premier Mai* or Michael Leiris' *Miroir de la Tauromachie* attest. Once the ritual of dressing is completed, tradition has it that the torero prays for a few moments in front of a small, portable altar. Bullfighters are more aware today than in the past of the symbolism and puzzling ambiguity of their role, both erotic and sacerdotal. They no longer speak so casually about the "orgasmic pleasure of the 'faena'." Some, like Esplá, are outraged by any public mention of this ambiguity. The mythical role they play in the ring is an intrinsic part of their indentity.

It seems that the quest for dignity that the Spanish people began more than two hundred years ago is culminating in a triumph of the metaphysical. Is this surprising for Spain? In this ascension, the suit has played a substantial role. At first merely the symbol of a social challenge that allowed a man to be as elegant as a noble, the suit has become, little by little, an end in itself, a precious object, a sculpture of gold and of light. An elaborate, routine ritual surrounds it, one that elevates both suit and wearer to the boundaries of the sacred.

Triptych:

Joselito and his "cuadrilla."

Overleaf:

Pepe Luis Vásquez (Sr.) in front of a portrait of himself when he was a bullfighter.

As the arena empties, one is struck by the calm of the crowd after the general excitement of the event. There are never violent outbreaks after a bullfight; the catharsis has already occurred! Over a hundred years ago, a French traveler by the name of Edgar Quinet gave an account of the feelings that overcame him in the deserted arena:
"I am alone, glued to my seat, my every limb feverish. The combination of murder, grace, enchantment, and dance has left me overwhelmed, dazed [...] I hear the roars and the dreams [...]. Never before has a dream brought me so quickly to the two extremes of infinity. This show, so strongly rooted in tradition, is not entertainment. It is an institution. It clings to the very heart and spirit of these people. It gets stronger, bolder; it never tires. It is possible that the strong characteristics of the Spanish people are maintained by emulating the bull, by composure, tenacity, heroism, by a disdain for death. In the legends of the North, Siegfried bathed in monster's blood in order to be invincible. Neither the spirit from the South of France, nor the gallantry of the Moors, nor the monarchy has been able to weaken Spain since it was shown the lessons of the Centaur."

Now we can only hope these same lessons are something that Spain will never foget.

José María Manzanares
wrapped in a "capote de paseo."

Acknowledgments.

Antonio Chenel "Antoñete"
Julio Aparicio (Sr.)
Miguel Flores
Fermín López
Pedrucho de Canarias
Enrique Bernedo "Bojilla"
Richard Milian
José Ortega Cano
Ricardo Ortiz
José Castilla
José Alba Cotón
Antonio Borrero "Chamaco"
Juan Bellido "Chocolate"
Pepe Luis Vásquez
Víctor Méndes
Pedrito de Portugal
Antonio José Galán
M. Espinosa "Armillita"
Jesús Pérez "El Madrileño"
Julio Aparicio
Pepe Luis Martín
Angel Luis Bienvenida
Julio Robles
Antonio Borrero "Chamaco" (Sr.)
Joselito and his "cuadrilla"
Juan Mora
Rui Bento
Morenito de Maracay and his
"cuadrilla"
Miguel Báez "Litri" (Sr.)
Sebastián Palomo Linares
Pepe Ibáñez
J. Antonio Ruiz "Espartaco" and
his "cuadrilla"
Rafael Corbelle
Luis Francisco Esplá
Davis Luguillano
José María Manzanares
Luis Miguel Dominguín
Enrique Ponce and his "cuadrilla"
Rafael Atienza
Manuel Atienza
Manuel Benítez "El Cordobés"
Juan Serrano "Finito de Córdoba"

Vincente Yesteras
Santiago Martín "El Viti"
César Rincón and his "cuadrilla"
Fernando Lozano
Antonio López

Jean and Dominique Bousquet
The city of Nîmes
Daniel Jean Valade
Françoise Lacassagne
Henri Westphal
Guy Tossato
Armelle Glavany
Chantal Charpentier
Danièle Carbonel
Sabine Arvieux
Christiane Buchet
Catherine Couton Mazet
Manuel Perez del Arco
Alice de Jenlis
Sébastien Ratto Viviani

"Los Borrachos de Velásquez"
restaurant
Carmen Navarro
Anemie Moulhusen
Ursula and Alex Henkes
Freddy Frisuelos
Canal +
Santiago García
Caja de Madrid
Lowe FMS
Ediciones Vogue España
Francisco Rafael Rodríguez
José Antonio Mérida
José Arias
Banco de Andalucía
As well as all the bullfighters'
agents.

Concept:
Peter Müller

Photographs:
Peter Müller

Assistants:
Curro Fito
Karla Christine Shelton
Javier Penado

Text:
Danièle Carbonel
Pedro Solèr
Fermín López

Preface:
Luis Miguel Dominguín

Translation (French to English):
Molly Stevens

Design and Creative Director:
Urs Frick

Art Director:
Javier Jiménez García

Production:
Picante Productions
The Fermín Studios

Photography Equipment:
Cameras and lenses by Hasselblad
Kodak film, Ektachrome 64

Light:
Broncolor

Laboratories :
As Color
Copyfoto
B/N Pepe Frisuelos.

Printed and bound by:
G. Canale & C . Italy

Photo-engraving:
Gravor SA Switzerland

© Assouline
26-28, rue Danielle Casanova - 75002 Paris - France
Tel. : +33 1 42 60 33 84 Fax : +33 1 42 60 33 85
http://www.imaginet.fr/assouline

First published in France by Editions Assouline, 1994
Oro Plata. Habits de lumière

Copyright for the text © 1994, Editions Assouline
English translation © 1997, Editions Assouline

Distributed to the U.S. trade by ST. MARTIN'S PRESS, New York
Distributed in Canada by McCLELLAND & STEWART
Distributed in all other countries, excluding France, Belgium and
Luxembourg by THAMES AND HUDSON (DISTRIBUTORS) LTD., London

ISBN 2-84323-035-7